5-07

Fact Finders™

Questions and Answers: Countries

Japan

A Question and Answer Book

by Michael Burgan

Consultant:
Dr. H. Todd Stradford
Department of Geography / Geology
University of Wisconsin-Platteville
Platteville, Wisconsin

Capstone
press

Mankato, Minnesota

Fact Finders is published by Capstone Press,
151 Good Counsel Drive, P.O. Box 669, Mankato, Minnesota 56002.
www.capstonepress.com

Library of Congress Cataloging-in-Publication Data
Burgan, Michael.
    Japan: a question and answer book / by Michael Burgan.
    p. cm.—(Fact finders. Questions and answers: countries)
    Includes bibliographical references and index.
    ISBN 0-7368-2478-2 (hardcover)
    1. Japan—Juvenile literature. I. Title. II. Series.
DS806.B83 2005b
952—dc22   2004021862

Summary: A brief introduction to Japan, following a simple question-and-answer format that
    discusses land features, government, housing, transportation, industries, education,
    sports, art forms, holidays, food, and family life. Includes a map, fast facts, and charts.

Editorial Credits
Megan Schoeneberger, editor; Kia Adams, series designer; Jennifer Bergstrom, book designer;
    maps.com, map illustrator; Wanda Winch, photo researcher; Scott Thoms, photo editor;
    Eric Kudalis, product planning editor

Photo Credits
Bruce Coleman Inc./David Madison, 12–13; Bruce Coleman Inc./James Montgomery, 19;
Capstone Press Archives, 29 (top); Corbis/AFP, 8–9; Corbis/Bettmann, 7; Corbis/John
Dakers/Eye Ubiquitous, 23; Corbis Saba/Tom Wagner, 16–17; Corbis/Walter Hodges, 21;
Corel, cover (background); Craig Lovell, 11; Folio Inc./Cynthia Foster, cover (foreground);
Photo courtesy of Suzanne Marlay, 24 (left); Photodisc/PhotoLink, 4, 14–15; PhotoSphere, 1;
Richard T. Nowitz, 24–25; Stockhaus Limited, 29 (bottom); Wolfgang Kaehler, 27

Artistic Effects
Capstone Press, 18 (logo); Ingram Publishing, 16 (left)

1 2 3 4 5 6 09 08 07 06 05

Table of Contents

Features

Where is Japan?

Japan is a chain of almost 4,000 islands in the Pacific Ocean. Together, the islands are slightly smaller than the U.S. state of California. Japan's largest island is Honshu. The other major islands are Kyushu, Shikoku, and Hokkaido.

The snow on Mount Fuji's peak melts in summer. ▶

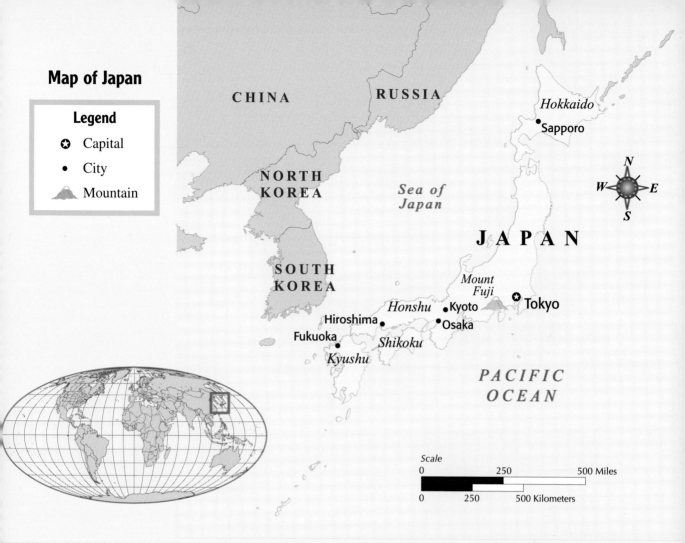

Map of Japan

Legend
- ✪ Capital
- • City
- 🏔 Mountain

CHINA

RUSSIA

Hokkaido
• Sapporo

NORTH KOREA

Sea of Japan

SOUTH KOREA

JAPAN

Mount Fuji

Honshu • Kyoto
Hiroshima • • Osaka
Fukuoka • Shikoku
Kyushu

✪ Tokyo

PACIFIC OCEAN

Scale
0 — 250 — 500 Miles
0 — 250 — 500 Kilometers

N W E S

Mountains are Japan's main landform. They cover most of Japan. The tallest peak is Mount Fuji, at 12,387 feet (3,776 meters). Many Japanese mountains are volcanoes. Earthquakes often occur near volcanoes. Each year, Japan has more than 1,000 earthquakes.

When did Japan become a country?

Japan became a country in 701. In that year, leaders started a new government. It was based on China's government. The city of Nara became the capital. In 794, Japan's leaders moved the capital to Kyoto.

In the 1500s, a civil war began. Japan's central government lost power. Local leaders ruled parts of Japan. In 1601, Tokugawa Ieyasu reunited the country. He became the military leader, or shogun, of all of Japan. His family ruled Japan for almost 270 years.

Fact!

Emperor Meiji moved the capital from Kyoto to Tokyo in 1868.

Emperor Meiji helped Japan become a stronger country.

On January 3, 1868, **Emperor** Meiji took control of Japan. He sent study groups to learn about schools, governments, and businesses in other countries. Emperor Meiji used the new information to develop Japan. In 1889, leaders wrote Japan's first **constitution**.

What type of government does Japan have?

Japan has a National **Diet** and a **prime minister**. Voters elect people to the National Diet. The Diet makes Japan's laws.

The Diet has two parts. The House of Representatives has 480 members. The House of Councillors has 252 members.

The Diet chooses one of its members to be prime minister. This person leads the country.

Fact!

After Japan's defeat in World War II (1939–1945), U.S. leaders rewrote Japan's constitution. The new constitution bans Japan from entering any wars except to defend its homeland.

Japan's lawmakers meet in a large group called the National Diet.

Japan still has an emperor. The emperor is a symbol of Japan's long history. Many Japanese also think of him as the father of all Japanese people. But he does not make laws or decisions for the country. He has only a few official jobs.

What kind of housing does Japan have?

Japanese people live in apartments or houses. In large cities, many people live in high-rise apartment buildings. Houses in cities are small and high priced. In the country, houses are cheaper.

Where do people in Japan live?

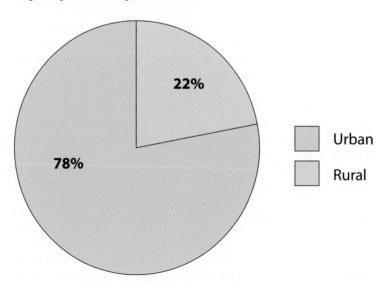

22%

78%

Urban

Rural

Japanese homes often have low tables, sliding panels, and straw mats.

Traditional Japanese homes differ from modern homes. Traditional homes have sliding wood panels instead of walls. The panels move to change the size of the rooms. Straw mats called tatami cover the floors. Modern Japanese homes have carpet and solid walls.

What are Japan's forms of transportation?

Many Japanese people use cars. Japan has about 72 million cars and trucks. Roads cost a lot of money to build in Japan. The roads must last through earthquakes.

Japan also has high-speed trains. The most famous train is called the Shinkansen. It travels at 180 miles (290 kilometers) per hour. It sometimes is called a bullet train.

Fact!

The world's longest train tunnel connects the islands of Honshu and Hokkaido. The Doraemon train uses the tunnel. Its name comes from a cartoon character, which is painted on the sides of the cars.

City streets in Japan are busy and crowded.

Besides cars and trains, some people use airplanes. Narita Airport in Tokyo is one of the busiest airports in Asia. At least 400 flights take off and land each day.

What are Japan's major industries?

Japanese people offer services, make products, and grow food. Most people work in businesses that offer services. Banking is important in Japan. The country has some of the world's largest banks.

Japan also makes many products. Car companies, such as Honda and Toyota, are in Japan. Sony makes TVs and stereos. Other companies make computers and computer parts. Some Japanese companies also make clothing and chemicals for medicines.

What does Japan import and export?

Imports	Exports
food products	cars
fuels	chemicals
textiles	machinery

Many Japanese factories use robots instead of workers. Japan has more "working robots" than any other country.

Fishing and farming are other main industries. Fishing crews catch tuna, trout, and crabs in the ocean. Rice is the most important crop. Farmers also grow wheat, potatoes, and citrus fruits.

What is school like in Japan?

Japanese children start school when they are 6 years old. They go to elementary school for six years. They spend three years in middle school. Students learn Japanese, math, science, history, music, and crafts.

In Japan, the school year starts in April. Students have a break from late July through August. They have shorter breaks the rest of the year. Students usually do homework during their breaks.

Fact!

Most elementary and middle school students help clean their schools. Their chores include sweeping halls and rooms and picking up trash in the school yard.

Japanese students have to work very hard in school.

After middle school, most Japanese students go to high school. They must pass a test to get into the school. To prepare for this test, some students go to a private school called a *juku*.

17

What are Japan's favorite sports and games?

Baseball is the most popular team sport in Japan. The country has 12 pro baseball teams. Many Japanese children play Little League baseball.

The favorite traditional sport in Japan is sumo wrestling. This form of wrestling was created in Japan hundreds of years ago. Most sumo wrestlers weigh between 220 and 330 pounds (100 and 150 kilograms). Sumo matches often last less than six seconds.

Fact!

Japan has won more than 300 Olympic medals.

Sumo wrestlers face off against each other in a match.

Shogi is a popular Japanese board game similar to chess or checkers. Players move flat wooden chips on a board. Some *shogi* games are shown on TV.

What are the traditional art forms in Japan?

Japan's traditional art forms include origami. Origami is the art of folding paper into shapes. Some origami shapes are simple. They can be made with just one piece of paper. Other origami art uses several pieces of paper.

Ikebana is the art of arranging flowers. Japan has more than 2,000 different styles of ikebana. People study for many years to learn the details of a style.

Fact!

Murasaki Shikibu wrote a book called The Tale of the Genji *during the early 1000s. Some scholars think it is the world's first novel.*

People fold colorful pieces of paper to make origami.

Haiku is one type of Japanese poetry. Each haiku has three lines. The first and third lines have five **syllables**. The second line has seven syllables.

What major holidays do people in Japan celebrate?

New Year's Day is one of Japan's major holidays. It is celebrated over several days. People prepare for New Year's Day by cleaning their homes. On New Year's Day, people eat a special meal. It includes fish cakes, mushrooms, and vegetables. People send each other cards. Children receive gifts from adults.

What other holidays do people in Japan celebrate?

Adult's Day
Children's Day
Emperor's Birthday
Respect for the Aged Day

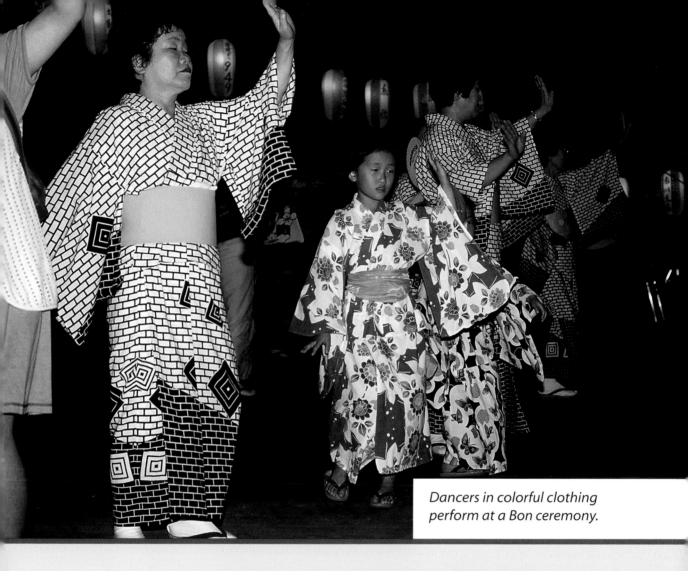

Dancers in colorful clothing perform at a Bon ceremony.

Another major holiday is Bon. It is a summer festival that honors the dead. During Bon, families visit the graves of their relatives. At the end of the festival, people often dance to traditional music. Friends and family members also give each other small gifts during Bon.

What are the traditional foods of Japan?

Fish, rice, and soybeans are traditional Japanese foods. Fish is often eaten raw in Japan. It is also grilled or dried.

Rice is a common food in Japan. Sushi is a type of rice made with **vinegar**. Sushi is served many ways. It is sometimes served with raw fish and a spicy spread called wasabi. Another type of sushi has eggs on top.

Fact!

The Japanese sometimes serve their food in a bento box. This box has several small sections to hold different kinds of food.

The Japanese often eat soup with their meals.

Soybeans are used to make tofu. Japanese people use this soft white food in soups. Japanese cooks use soybeans to make a paste called miso. Miso cooked in soup is a popular meal. People also eat soybeans straight from the pod.

25

What is family life like in Japan?

In the past, most Japanese families included many relatives living together. Today, most families have only parents and their children in one house. Elderly people often live alone.

What are the ethnic backgrounds of people in Japan?

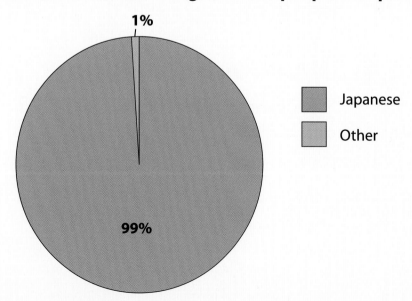

1%

99%

Japanese

Other

Japanese families enjoy spending time together.

Today, many families are busy. They have less time to eat together at home. But many families still make time to dine out and travel together.

Japan Fast Facts

Official name:

Japan

Land area:

145,882 square miles
(377,834 square kilometers)

**Average annual
precipitation (Tokyo):**

55 inches (140 centimeters)

**Average January
temperature (Tokyo):**

38 degrees Fahrenheit
(3 degrees Celsius)

**Average July temperature
(Tokyo):**

77 degrees Fahrenheit
(25 degrees Celsius)

Population:

127,214,499 people

Capital city:

Tokyo

Language:

Japanese

Natural resources:

water, forests, coal

Religions:

both Shinto and Buddhist   84%
other   16%

Money and Flag

Money:

Japan's money is called the yen. In 2004, 1 U.S. dollar equaled 106.25 yen. One Canadian dollar equaled 83.4 yen.

Flag:

Japan's flag is white with a red circle in the center. The circle stands for the sun. The Japanese sometimes call their country "the Land of the Rising Sun."

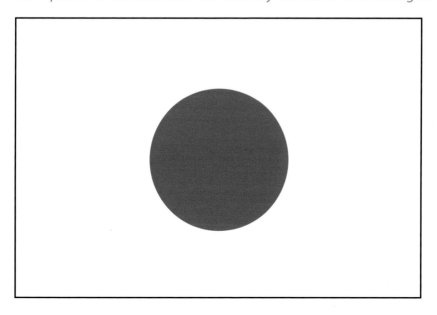

Learn to Speak Japanese

To write their language, the Japanese do not use letters like the ones in English. Instead, they draw small images called characters. Some words can be written with a single character. Here are some Japanese words written with the English alphabet.

English	Japanese	Pronunciation
hello	kon ni chi wa	(koh-NEE-chee-wah)
see you later	ato de	(a toh day)
yes	ha i	(HYE)
no	i i e	(EE-ay)
please	o ne gai shi ma su	(oh-nay-GUY shee-MAH-soo)
thank you	do mo a ri ga tou	(DOH-moh ah-ree-GAH-toh)
excuse me	su mi ma sen	(soo-mee-mah-sen)

Glossary

constitution (kon-stuh-TOO-shuhn)—the written system of laws in a country that state the rights of the people and the power of government

diet (DYE-uht)—the group of people who have been elected to make laws in some countries

emperor (EM-pur-ur)—the male ruler of an area called an empire

prime minister (PRIME MIN-uh-stur)—the person in charge of a government in some countries

syllable (SIL-uh-buhl)—a unit of sound in a word

vinegar (VIN-uh-gur)—a sour liquid used to preserve food and add flavor

Internet Sites

FactHound offers a safe, fun way to find Internet sites related to this book. All of the sites on FactHound have been researched by our staff.

Here's how:
1. Visit *www.facthound.com*
2. Type in this special code **0736824782** for age-appropriate sites. Or enter a search word related to this book for a more general search.
3. Click on the **Fetch It** button.

FactHound will fetch the best sites for you!

Read More

Costain, Meredith, and Paul Collins. *Welcome to Japan.* Countries of the World. Philadelphia: Chelsea House, 2001.

DeAngelis, Gina. *Japan.* Many Cultures, One World. Mankato, Minn.: Capstone Press, 2003.

Guile, Melanie. *Japan.* Culture In. Chicago: Raintree, 2004.

Thomas, Mark. *The Seikan Railroad Tunnel: World's Longest Tunnel.* Reading Power. New York: PowerKids Press, 2002.

Index